THE
MANDALA FLOWERS
COLORING BOOK

THE
MANDALA FLOWERS
COLORING BOOK

David Woodroffe

SIRIUS

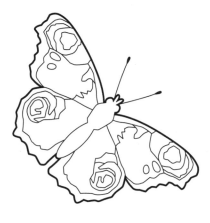

SIRIUS

This edition published in 2023 by Sirius Publishing, a division of
Arcturus Publishing Limited,
26/27 Bickels Yard, 151–153 Bermondsey Street,
London SE1 3HA

ISBN: 978-1-3988-3023-3
CH011210NT
Supplier 29, Date 0723, PI 00003894

Printed in China

Introduction

Mandalas are geometric configurations of symbols that are used in a number of eastern religions, including Hinduism, Buddhism, Jainism, and Shinto. They represent variously a map of deities, paradises, an ideal universe, and in Shinto, actual shrines. They may be used as tools of spiritual guidance, for meditation, and for creating a sacred space.

In some traditions, mandalas are painted on scrolls and carried by travelers. They represent the spiritual journey, starting from the outside and working through a series of different layers to the core.

With their delicate petals and graceful stems, flowers are the perfect medium to create a beautiful set of unique mandalas. This collection of images contains delightful designs that draw you in with mesmerizing floral patterns. Some are composed of a collage of flowers, while other mandalas are themselves a complete flower.

Whether you are a lover of floral designs or addicted to mandalas, pick a design that appeals to you, grab your favorite set of coloring pencils, pens, or markers and enter the state of peace and concentration that comes with coloring. It's the perfect way to relax and calm your mind after a long day.

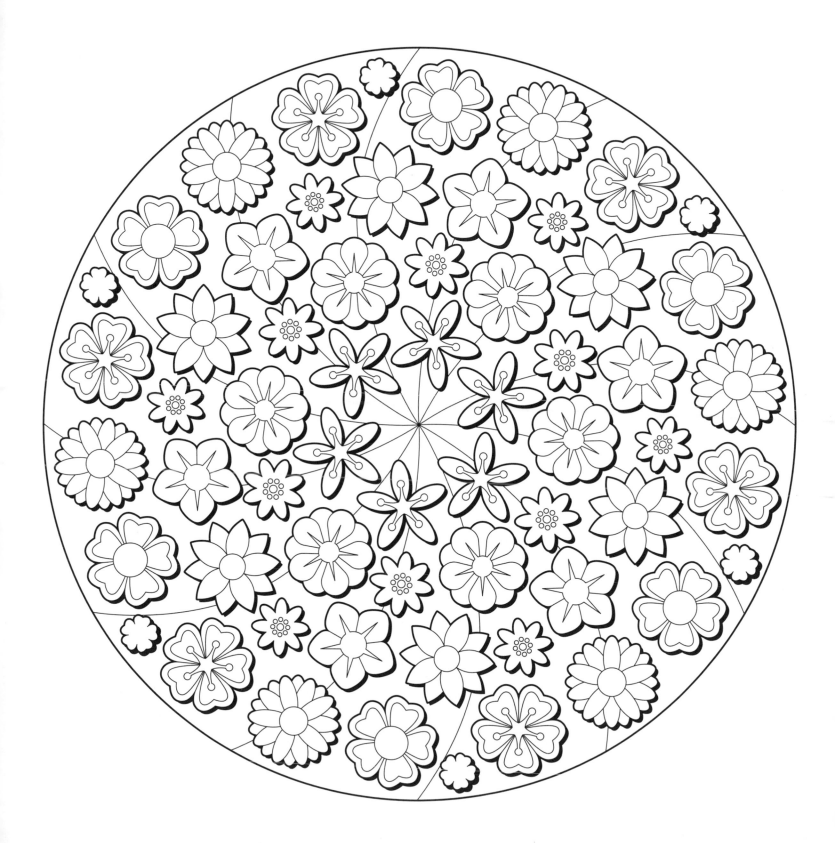

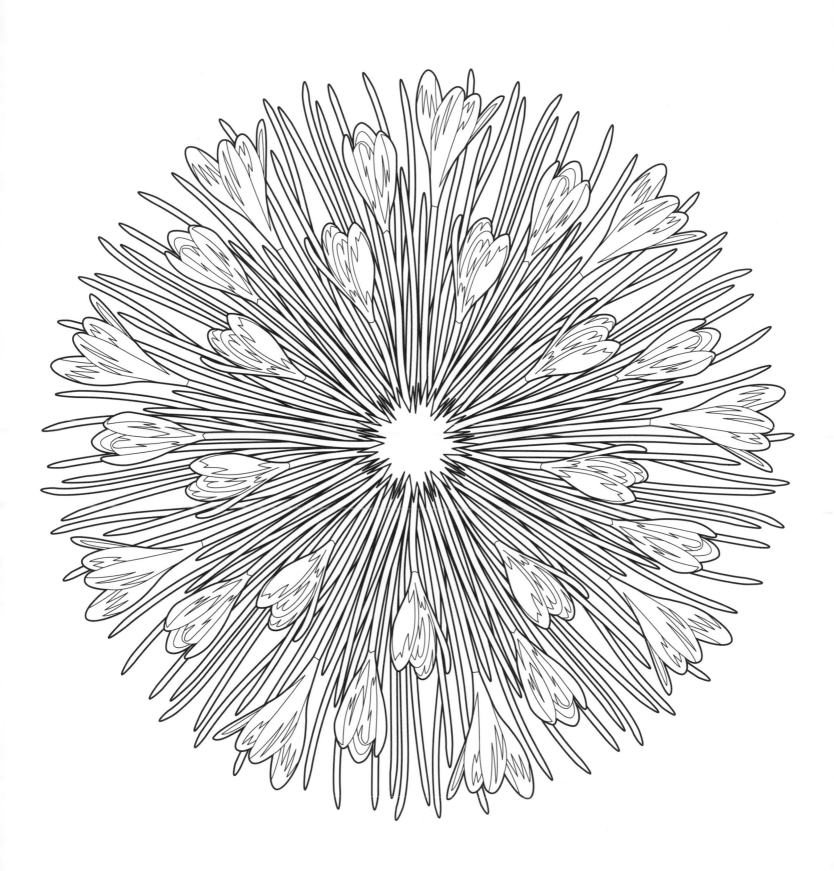

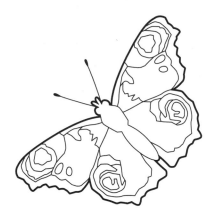
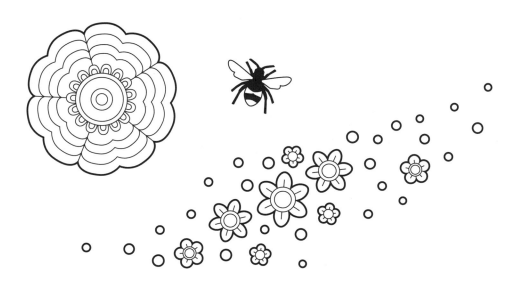